*Obsequy
for Lost Things*

Martin Anderson

Obsequy
for Lost Things

Shearsman Books

First published in the United Kingdom in 2014 by
Shearsman Books
50 Westons Hill Drive
Emersons Green
BRISTOL
BS16 7DF

Shearsman Books Ltd Registered Office
30–31 St. James Place, Mangotsfield, Bristol BS16 9JB
(this address not for correspondence)

www.shearsman.com

ISBN 978-1-84861-350-8

ACKNOWLEDGEMENTS
The Lower Reaches first appeared, in different form,
as a chapbook from Shearsman Books in 2013.
In the Year of Expeditions first appeared in
Shearsman magazine, nº 99/100 (2014).

Cover illustration by Donald Maxwell,
from his book *Unknown Essex* (1925).

Contents

"It is only delusion, and not knowledge,
that bestows happiness."

Stefan Zweig

THE LOWER REACHES

"This is England, and I'm in a nice, clean English room with all the dirt swept under the bed."

Jean Rhys

ONE

I

After the high pitched whine of bellicosity: "We'll bomb you back to the stone age" the remote is pressed. Crackle of distressed air. Warm, incendiary smell. All colour implodes to a white mote. Silence. The crevasse opens.

II

Boiling white spume. Caught on steps of the public baths before noon, the shadow of a vapour. Ash, in the dissolved hand. Shard, or ember. All melted into air. In the stone, heart's cold memento.

III

What keel breaks this ice? What *dignitas* is affirmed in these particulars of a profound winter? Our Lady of the Salterns bless this rotting wharf, this ramshackle back-end deserted by the tides. It is snowing over all the reed clogged wet-lands of the earth.

IV

Scent of sea asters edged the creek. "Die Tankanlagen" under the aimer's sight. "Marschland." Identified/located from a great height. Locked in a grid: "Zu den Sachen selbst!" Held for a moment in his gaze, they bled. Blackened viscera. The air received them.

V

Outside the window purple reeded hollows of the former channel. Sea lavender, grey with river light. At the inlet's mouth. There, where a "leakinge, unwholesome ship" once harvested wind, tide lapped silt bars catching the sun's last rays ignite. As, too, the scarp's high ledge of flowering thorn – a "Sea-mark", Hawkesbury-bush > Hamechesburga > burh: *hill*. The Hill of the Hawks. To navigate a way back, from the farthest corners of the earth.

VI

Togodumnus. Dead or lost amidst the reed beds. Harried from fen to fen. His horses slain. Pursued into the claggy wastes east of the Island of Thorns. Aiming beyond the sand capped wooded heights for Camulodunum, he disappeared. Sound of the bittern booming amid bull rushes. Slither of sword hilt and shield, as each man sought to hold his footing through the miry labyrinth. Water welded to sky. On the salt driven wind the sound of men closing. Panick, then stumbling. A foreign tongue. There is gold in Dalcouthi. There is silver.

VII

Over the mudflats the smell of oil. Dream of an ideal order.
Beyond any particular geography, any particular time or place
at all. Driving men mad. Blacking the shore. Leveraging the sea-
lanes open. "A perpetuall warre without peace or truce." Crude.
Pungent in summer, over the fields and hedgerows. And in the
houses of the villages. Ancient distillate. Of a mind which "(save
upward to the heavens) could have little solace or content in
respecte of any outward objects." Or any inward excursus.

TWO

I

Out of the forlorn city at last, its fogs and its counting houses. The white noise in the rigging after dark. Droning. Insincere. Incessant. Past Thorn Island where one summer the effluvium became too much even for those inside debating. Each voice overlapping and merging with the other. And with those outside, reporting. Downstream. Past Hole Haven. Scent of sea lavender on the breeze. White noise in the rigging. Smell of the open sea roads. Stars look down on another journey about to be undertaken.

II

Struggling through deep drifts with a copy of *Der Angriff* under his arm, a latter-day Robert Conway. Ice fragments from the Pontic steppes lodged deep in the tread of his boots, his shadow survives in abattoirs and in the stockyards of railway terminuses. In the frozen breath of *die Kristallnacht*. But who has not followed and extolled, through a bloodied swathe of foreign villages and towns, that small red rowan on his cheek, "that nobly arched head, containing such a quantity of brain … those coral lips?"

III

Driftway, sluice. Beyond, breakwater, river scour, margin. Where foreland of saltern is over-lapped. "All overflowen". And eyot, and terp: "quite drowned". No tithe map. No tiltboat to stairs or wharf. Undrained. Unforded. What soggy track, inter-coursed with copse/willow, to follow? All wet-land words, and ways, converge; seem foreign. To find a way, amid shifting brine sump, piling, hollow.

IV

Togodumnus. Feet in mud. Following the channel's curve. Seeking the higher ground. Above the sedge lapped verge his shadow flits. Gulls cry out over the sunken tideway. Revenge. But there are no tracks to guide him back. Each imprint erased in the flood's quiet launder.

V

For "a pug nosed rodent with lustrous fur", for a pile of moth-eaten pelts, the "beaver fields exhausted", the great Eastern deciduous forest depleted, a civilisation, with no concept of wealth accumulation, "debauched".

VI

Shiver and sweat of tidewrack. Limbs blue. Cold flicker on silt bank. Slippage of foot. Through Flat and Ooze. Where the river "enters the Ocean" – "carelessly camped upon its bank". *In avia secutus.* Head spun. Heart colder. To bend, finally, at Claudius' foot. Not dead. A survivor. REG MAG IN BRIT. An instrument, *reges et amici*, of the imperium. Benefactor, and supporter, of an ideal order.

VII

Sun dappled worm-eaten wharf in a wilderness of water and sky. Where the "aguish miasma" rose after sun dip. Where the starch collared pilot set out under the sand capped scarp. Light on hedgebank, on fill dyke. To guide far off destinies afloat through treacherous shoals, sands. For a country intent, at any cost, on extending its reach. *Oppidum*. Power point. Wooden pile driven into the mud.

VIII

"Big swinging dicks" amid the rigging. All hands below aloft chipping ice off a top heavy vessel. The ice-master frantic. All LIBOR rates "fixed". "A ... culture rotten with cynicism and greed." From the Hill of the Hawks, what eye looks down?

IX

A journey endlessly postponed. In the leather lined clubs of its capital. At regattas, tattoos and royal enclosure. In "cultivate[d] nostalgia". In the Honours list nailed to the door. In expurgated diaries of heros who "swear all day at [their] companions" and are transformed into "splendid failure[s]". In 'lost' government archives. In the inherited and laundered loot of families and State. In a mythos of fairness assiduously cultivated and disposed. By an emasculated corps of vendors of 'news'. By a plethora of anointed insouciants.

X

From le Hole havene, "in very deep and current free water at maximum practicable distance from the coast ... the files ... in weighted crates", *And specially from every shires ende / Of Engelond ... they wende* past gut and hedgebank, creekside and shore, on "perambulation", prayers offered en route, pollard "bounds trees" freshly scored or mutilated, on occasion youths ceremoniously scourged so they would remember a significant location, "by the time I cut his balls off ... he had no ears and his eyeball, the right one, I think, was hanging out of its socket", mapping the "Bounds of the parish". Three and a half tons of what "might embarrass" the government, and "whose existence ... should never be revealed". Scent of sea lavender over the mud. "...he died before we got much out of him". Smell of the open sea roads.

XI

Our Lady of the Salterns bless this rotting wharf, this ramshackle back-end deserted by the tides.

IN THE YEAR
OF EXPEDITIONS

"We are filled with homesickness for no identifiable home."
James Hamilton-Paterson

Interlocutors of pure silences, and of snows. On a still night. What eye's afloat. What heart's adrift. Upon a fragment. A phantom.

From swampy, tide-washed wild flower salterns where the creek once bent by Lady's Island, poling with long oars up torturous narrows.

In our minds that "implacable blancheur"; unmapped, untrodden. Illimitable waste. Flower of a cold lattice, on which the wave breaks.

Across the horizon History marches. Shadows weep. From the Archive of Paradise a rare bird. In its beak – exquisite plumage! – bright petals. We sought warmth in the ashes of their extinguished fires.

An expedition of vanishings. Air beaten to airy thinness. From the alembic of the Word flesh and bone excised. Each thing that we extolled we removed. A fragrance hung on the world.

At night in our dreams a strange figure came toward us. Then stopped. From the alder swamp by the dim light of the creek head it waved. It pronounced upon us all the blessings of whiteness.

And Joas Croppenburgh, and Giles Vanderputt, held back the sea for us. Day after day we heard, amidst sallow willow in the deep field ditch, it rage.

Over their ruined roads and villages only phantoms returned. With no memories.

Not even in the midnight cry of love tangling the high balustrade – filigree fragrance! – does there float an uncontaminated moment.

Suddenly one night in our dreams she turned up. Unannounced. Forgotten. To claim, she said, all the gods, and all the songs, we had taken from her.

A new land, smelling sweeter than all the rest. The small boat we put over the side, to claim it. The exclamations of astonishment. What the wave brought back. The Chimera's gaze. The haunting artefact of loss.

In the penumbra's liquid throat. A hoarse aubade. Note flung out over settlements of stones and charcoal. A settled gloom. What ear, before dark, will hear that voice, before it is gone forever?

It is snowing. Over all the horizons of the dead the wind has fallen silent. The arquebuses dissolved. It is snowing, in the canyons of the blind where all the codices have been wiped clean. In the silence the pure fire of a crystal burns. No one leaves any footprints. No one arrives or departs.

Through damp backlands, where ditch side reed was in season, by old Dutch embankments, by steadings where hazel and dogwood loomed lush and full, by Marsh bailiff Zacharia Button's cottage, in the Year of Expeditions.

We searched for her. On the polluted tideway. Soured with salt. A wave breaking, always further off. Effigy. Rubbing. Our "Ladie of the sea". Slipping, always, from us. Scent, of that pure point-instant adrift on the word. That we pursue in our dreams. That our dreams pursue when we wake.

No journey's end. No end to looking. But under the moon we raised up a giant gallows. Harvested pain. We sharpened our blades upon them.

All the names erased – from plinth and citadel. The salt eaten into them. The vestige of a world returned to silence. They were "Sojourners in the land" only. The un-cognised. Inheriting the Ocean.

The sea runs in us its incendiary course.

From the occluded depth of crystal in the steaming brine pan this sifted alabaster, asperged. Sea's lace. Sea's breath. Through whose freshet of lattices will dissolve, again, its unexpungeable vapours, endlessly protean phantasms and shadows.

Can you not hear, can you not smell these shadows jostling with their rotting cadence through a skin of depredations. Inscribed on the bones of the living, and the dead. Distempered, draped in a shroud. Entering the graveyard?

Murmurings, expostulations in the dark. But the orders have been promulgated. The street names changed. No evidence, no signs of a crime committed. All outward destinations are the same.

Whorled in the force of their going, torque of a name whose sound no longer exists except as another, deeply inscribed space whose signature is a wave alternating, overlapping, combining, upon which rises and sinks the inexhaustible flotsam of days.

On a still night, a sonorous chorus of birds. Roosting harmonies. Feather, moss lined dreams. The window's flickering lamp accentuates shadows within.

It is snowing. The air seeded with blossom. We stir in rooms above courtyards where the fountains have frozen. Stir to the shear cry of a gull driven by the sea's raging. A haunting cry wreathed in the high wrought balconies between sleep and waking. A cry reminding us of home.

When will the corn ripen again on the rises above the grey saltern's edges. Its shadow wave in the breeze. Beyond, above high perched Hawkesbury, in the rain that falls without stopping, day after day after day. Where stalk and root rot in the ground and a malodorousness through the black earth continually oozes?

In the snow only the wind knows the names of those who are always weightless, who are always disappearing.

OBSEQUY FOR LOST THINGS

"The weather of these northern districts is so changeable
that, even with my experience, it is impossible
to foretell the sky of tomorrow"

Matsuo Bashō

In these white, unhypostasized spaces a bird sings. Above a frozen river. It is neither evening, nor morning. Ancient, valedictory syllabaries whisper on the wind.

All the borders are closed. Or dissolved. No more promiscuously trafficking across them. And all the signposts are buried, or are pointing the wrong way.

Sound of the tongue on these crisp, ice fringed margins. The rustle of the page is not as loud as the silence of the departed.

No voice, here, emits a call for the mounting of an expedition. The dead hussar, enshrined in the glass of the glacier, is pointing his horse toward a dark cloud on the horizon shaped like a spectre.

Scratched with a nail, in irrefrangible crystal, a name: "..... ..... was here." But, in this air of invincible whiteness, no locus exists. Either spatial or temporal. And all the writing on the wall is upside down. The world spelled backwards.

The silence drifts. Across the frozen river the sound of a bird. In the geography of all absent things things that are about to appear are forgotten.

On a road a man is counting the flakes of snow in his beard. Above, clouds of grey are massing. Confused by the snow, like a subject momentarily bereft of a sentence, he struggles as it becomes a blizzard to find his way home.

It is neither morning, nor evening. It is neither winter, nor summer; autumn nor spring.

Only later did they realise they had been walking backwards and forwards across the border without knowing it was there.

Everyone is walking, in worn out boots, back to a country they do not remember but which they have been exiled from.

In the "dissolved lodge" above the snow line. In a street with no one in it. In shuttered, empty rooms. The shadow of far off places. Tangier. Alaska. Sumatra. Somalia. The Moon.

Fear: of dis-possession. Of all that they are. Tottering above this abyss of etiolation, this border without a name swept by immense silences and distances.

Sounds, through the vast echo chamber of unresolved identities. Voices. Exiled amidst the fragments. The contingent, 'unreal' deposits of time.

Leaves rustle on tumuli. A "Barbikew" of bodies. Here everything is remembered. And everything is forgotten. In the "fathomless gulf of avarice" the border is drawn and re-drawn each minute, each hour.

Country of the lost. A sweating incubus is slowly devouring the night. The voices of those who "disappear" grow hoarse in the throats of the living. They have swallowed a blankness too large for them to bear.

To eliminate the antinomial > synthesize. Till you are left with *harmonie* > ... As if there can be affirmation without negation. Stillness without tension.

The land unploughed, unfenced. Hence "unpeopled", "vacant". No footprint was discerned. On the leafy sunlit ridge above the river. Sour Wood. Sumac. Buck-eye. The freedom of the unconstrained. Forsaking frontiers and borders for where there were none … Dark neurotica of a dream. Collective sweepings.

Voices, off frozen steppe. A "People without Space". Rose through the lean decades of hunger and of fear. Their wheel ruts were visible for miles. Across immense distances. Smoke from their campfires lingered for days, years.

"Merely apportion us some poor, unwanted designation," they implored, "a name." As if words, and names, were things. "We'll plant it, here, deep in the soil. When it grows we'll become the flesh of its sound, its home."

Snow falls. Indiscriminately across borders. Covering road, fence, field. Cancelling identities. White crystal cantor in whose freezing breath the unbuttressed takes flight. Obsequy for lost things.

Inside, prints of ferns on frosted panes. Door left half open. Broken chairs and trestle. Torn pages scattered over the floor. Outside, empty chicken coup. Kindling wood left in the lane. A silence not heard before.

Flurbereinigung. The geist of History incarnated. Footprints of a foul chimera in the mud. Assailed by voices. All the leaves have turned red. A bird sings deep in woods. It is snowing again – over roads and walls and fields. Over all the empty spaces.

No names, now, over the worn out roads. The washed out fields. Beside the protracted lengths of the journey. A journey to nowhere. On dusty verges, in roadside ditches small hands weave the rain into a repository of silence.

Exiled amidst the fragments, the contingent 'unreal' deposits of time, the light is forever changing. Is never "immobile". Disdaining, in each dawn grey window, the day the hour the minute the second of its endlessly coming and going.

A bird sings. Above a frozen river. It is neither morning, nor evening. It is snowing. It is neither summer nor winter, autumn nor spring.

NOTES

THE LOWER REACHES

ONE

I: "We'll bomb…", Pakistan's President Musharraf, BBC television interview, 2006. Threat made to him by US official. [First used by American General Curtis LeMay in 1968 in relation to N. Vietnam.]

IV: "Die…", from target photographs of the Thameshaven oil refineries on Fobbing marsh issued to Luftwaffe aircrews during WWII.
    "Zu den ..", Edmund Husserl, *Logische Untersuchungen*, 1900/01. [We must turn to the things themselves! – Rather than, as in Kant, the mystical thing-in-itself.]

V: "Outside the window…", following the great North Sea Flood of 1953, in which many people drowned, Fobbing's navigable tideway was, in the interests of safety, dammed off and its creek eventually dried out.
    "leakinge, unwholesome…", John Smith, *The Generall History of Virginia, New England, and the Summer Isles*, 1624: Smith's description is of the *Mayflower*.
    "Sea-mark", Randal Bingley, *Fobbing: Essays on an Essex Parish*.

VI: Togodumnus: a king of the Catuvellauni in southern England who, in a battle described as one of the most important in English history and which might have taken place between present-day East Tilbury and Stanford-le-Hope, resisted the Roman invasion/ occupation (CE43) and who was "lost" "retreating into trackless wastes" of the Essex marshes and became, Hind claims, a client king.

VII: "a perpetuall…", Virginia Company *Records* vol.1, 1622. [By 1685 the Powhatans of the Chesapeake tidelands were reportedly "extinct"].
    "(save upward…", William Bradford first Governor of Plymouth, New England, 1620, *Of Plymouth Plantation*.

TWO

I: "Hole Haven…", inlet on the Thames estuary "traditionally serving as a minor harbour for sea-going vessels" (Bingley). A place much visited, especially its *Lobster Smack Inn*, by the novelist Joseph Conrad's lifelong friend G.W.F. Hope, who along with Conrad lived at one time in Stanford-le-Hope, an Essex village on the banks of the Thames a couple of miles from Hole Haven. Hope, in his *Friend of Conrad* (1926), describes it: "The next day we went aboard the *Nellie*, taking with us a cold leg of lamb … we got down to the Lower Hope reach. We passed several sailing ships and steamers as we made our way down to Hole Haven. When we got near the Haven I told Conrad I would take the foresail in and to keep her well down to the sea wall so as not to run any risk of touching the spit as we approached the creek. We had a fair wind in, so I lowered the main sail and took in the mizzen. We then ran up above the jetty, and let go the anchor just inside the eel schoots. We then stowed the sails and brought forth the lamb". In Hope's manuscript he identifies himself as the "Director" in Conrad's *Heart of Darkness*, an extract from which precedes this description.

II: *Der Angriff*, newspaper published by Joseph Goebbels.
      Robert Conway, main protagonist in the Frank Capra film *Lost Horizon* 1937.
      "that nobly…", Charles White, *An Account of the Regular Graduations in Man*,1799 [White in his account was referring to Europeans].

V: "For a…", Eric J. Dolin, *Fur, Fortune and Empire*.
      "beaver fields…", *Jesuits Relations*, 1635 [from an estimated population of 60+ million beavers].

VI: This entire section indebted to J.F. Hind's *A Plautius' Campaign in Britain. An Alternative Reading of the Narrative in Cassius Dio (60.19.5-21.2)*
      "in avia…", retreating into trackless wastes, *op.cit.*
      "REG MAG…", Great King in Britain, *op.cit.*
      "reges et…", compliant, friendly kings, *op.cit.*

VII: "aguish miasma", William Gibbens, *The Essex Review*, 1902.

VIII: "Big swinging…", term denoting a successful financial-sector trader, and popularised by Michael Lewis in his partly-auto-biographical book, *Liar's Poker* (1989).

"A culture…", Adair Turner, Financial Services Authority, London, June 2012.

IX: "cultivated…", Eduardo Galeano, *Open Veins of Latin America*. ["The powerful who legitimate their privileges by heredity cultivate nostalgia."]

"swear all…", Roland Huntford, *Shackleton*. [Referring to Robert Falcon Scott].

X: "From le…", circa 1263, Randal Bingley, *op.cit.* [Hole Haven was also known as Holy Haven.]

"in very…", *National Archives*, United Kingdom. [Relating to "purged" Kenya files. Those involved in such purging were required to be "a British subject of *European descent*."] Italics mine.

"perambulation", Randal Bingley, *op.cit.*

"by the…", an unnamed settler of the *Kenyan Police Reserve* who participated in a Special Branch interrogation: "Stayed for a few hours to help the boys out, softening him up…". Interviewed and cited by C. Elkins, *Britain's Gulag: the Brutal End of Empire in Kenya*.

"Bounds of…", Randal Bingley, *op.cit.*

"might embarrass…", Ian MacLeod, UK Secretary of State for the Colonies, 1961.

"he died…", C.Elkins, *op.cit.*